A Crazy Collection of Jokes For Teachers

(c) 2018 Robert Frosdick

All rights reserved. No part of this publication may be reproduced, stored in a retrieval system or transmitted in any form without the prior written permission of the author.

Every effort has been made to ensure the contents of this book are correct at the time of publication. Nevertheless, the publisher cannot be held responsible for any errors or omissions, or for the consequences of any reliance on the information provided by the same. This does not affect your statutory rights.

If you would like to suggest jokes for inclusion or provide any other information please email feedback@nssales.co.uk

Teaching can sometimes be a stressful, demanding, thankless, underpaid, frustrating, monotonous, and demoralising task - but enough of the positives. We know how hard teachers work, so we think every now and again you deserve to sit back, put your feet up, relax and have a jolly good laugh and giggle.

This Crazy Collection of Jokes for Teachers contains nearly 200 hilarious jokes, quips, gags and one-liners all about schools and teaching. From the downright childish to the frankly rude, this side-splitting collection is sure to having to roaring with laughter... long enough to even temporarily forget about that pile of homework you have to grade!

So put the kettle on, make yourself comfortable, sit back and enjoy our crazy collection of riotous jokes.

CLASSROOM CLASSICS

Two boys were arguing when the teacher entered the room.

The teacher said, "Why are you arguing?"

One of the boys answered, "We found a ten pound note and decided to give it to whoever tells the biggest lie."

"You should be ashamed of yourselves," said the teacher, "When I was your age I didn't even know what a lie was."

The boys gave the ten pounds to the teacher.

The teacher is droning away in the classroom when he notices a student sleeping way up in the back row. The teacher shouts out to the class, "Hey wake that student up!"

A voice at the back replied "You put him to sleep, you wake him up!"

Student in the canteen: "Why is this chop so tough?"

School Cook: "Because it's a karate chop."

Student in the canteen: "There's is a fly in my soup!"

School Cook: "That's the meat."

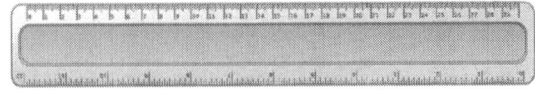

Teacher: "Annie, what's the chemical formula for water?"

Annie: "H I J K L M N O."

Teacher: "What are you talking about?"

Annie: "Didn't you say it's H to O?"

Did you hear about the chemistry teacher who told his class a joke. He got no reaction.

Teacher: "I wish you'd pay a little attention, David."

David: "Give me a break, I'm paying as little as I can."

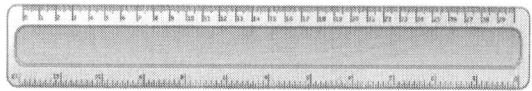

Miss. Johnson wrote on the chalk board, "I ain't had no fun all summer."

"So, George," she said. "What should I do to correct this?"

"Get a partner" George answered.

Teacher: "Joe, can you give me a sentence beginning with the letter I?"

Joe: "I is..."

Teacher (interrupting angrily): "Joe! How many more times do I have to tell you! You must always say 'I am...'"

Joe: "All right sir. How about this - I am the letter in the alphabet after H."

Teacher: "You missed school yesterday, didn't you?"

Student: "Not very much."

Student: "Can I go to the toilet?"

Teacher: "Only if you can say the alphabet."

Student: "Okay abcdefghijklmnoqrstuvwxyz"

Teacher: "Where's the p?"

Student: "Half way down my leg."

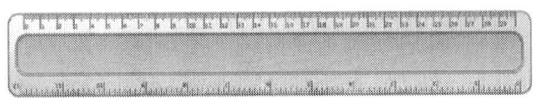

The school secretary answered the phone to be informed, "I'm phoning to tell you that Peter Smith is sick and won't be coming to school today."

The secretary replied "Oh, I am sorry to hear that. Can I just ask who is calling?"

The voice on the telephone replied, "This is my father."

Teacher: "Why are you talking during my lesson?"

Student: "Why are you teaching during my conversation?"

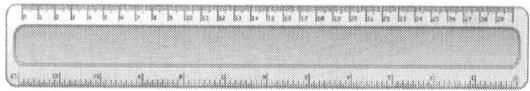

Teacher: "Simon, can you say your name backwards?"

Simon: "No Mis."

Mum: "What did you learn in school today?"

Son: "Not enough - I have to go back again tomorrow."

Son: "My math teacher is crazy".

Mother: "Why?"

Son: "Yesterday she told us that five is 4+1, now today she is telling us that five is 3 + 2."

A frog telephones the Psychic Hotline. His Personal Psychic Advisor tells him, "You are going to meet a beautiful young girl who will want to know everything about you."

The frog is thrilled, "This is great! Will I meet her at a party?"

"No," says his advisor, "in her biology class."

Teacher: "What is the formula for water?"

Student: "H, I, J, K, L, M, N, O"

Teacher: "That's not what I taught you."

Student: "But you said the formula for water was... H to O."

Father: "How do you like going to school?"

Son: "The going bit is fine, as is the coming home bit too, but I'm not too keen on the time in-between!"

Luke comes home from his first day of school, and his mother asks, "What did you learn today?"

"Not enough," Luke replies. "They said I have to go back tomorrow."

A teacher bumped into the cleaner one evening and decided to complain about the cleanliness of her classroom; "Look at the dust on my desk, it looks like it hasn't been cleaned for a fortnight!"

The cleaning lady replied "Well you can't blame me for that, I've only been here a week."

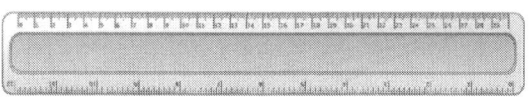

A sixth form student who had just learned to drive arrived at his mechanics class late, explaining to the teacher, "Sorry I'm late, I had water in the carburettor."

"Where is the car now?" the teacher replied.

"In the lake" the student explained.

A teacher takes a holiday to San Francisco. In her hotel room she opens the drawer, and there it was; Tony Bennett's heart.

I guess he left it there.

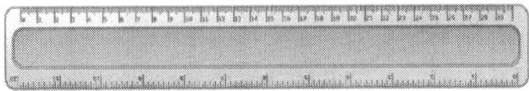

Student: "Sorry I'm late, I went to the dentist this morning."

Teacher: "Does your tooth still hurt?"

Student: "I don't know - the dentist kept it."

I was sitting next to a man on the bus and he kept saying "Call me a doctor, Call me a doctor!"

I asked him, "What's the matter, are you ill?"

"No," he replied "I just graduated from medical school."

A student bumps into a former teacher at a high school reunion. The student says to the teacher "I'm afraid I don't recall your face - but your breath is familiar.

Teacher: "Whoever answers my next question, can go home."

One student throws his bag out the window.

Teacher: "Who just threw that?!"

Student: "Me! I'm going home now."

An elderly teacher dies and leaves the shortest will ever. It says; "Being of sound mind, I spent all my money!"

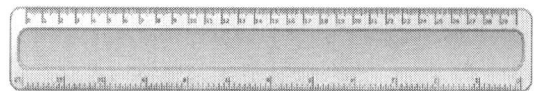

A junior teacher asked his senior colleague, who had been married for 30 years, what the secret of a long marriage was. The colleague explained, "We always take time to go to a restaurant twice a week - a little candlelight, dinner, soft music and dancing.... She goes Tuesdays, I go Fridays."

At the end of the class, a chemistry teacher asked her students what was the most important thing that they learned in the lesson.
A student promptly raised his hand and said, "Never lick the spoon."

Boy: "You're stupid and smelly!"

Girl: "Do you know who I am?"

Boy: "No."

Girl: "I'm the Head Teachers daughter."

Boy: "Do you know who I am?"

Girl: "No."

Boy: "Good." (walks away).

Did you hear about the teacher that yelled "F, YOU GUYS!" to her students.
Another perk of being a music teacher...

Teacher: "If a lion is chasing you, what would you do?"

Student: "I'd climb a tree."

Teacher: "If the lion climbs a tree?"

Student: "I will jump in the lake and swim."

Teacher: "If the lion also jumps in the water and swims after you?"

Student: "Just who's side are you on here?"

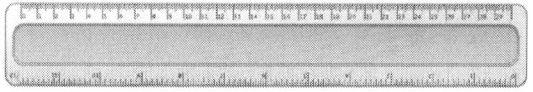

Teacher: "Why are you late to class, Kate?"

Kate: "Because of a sign down the road."

Teacher: "What does a sign have to do with your being late?"

Kate: "The sign said, 'School Ahead, Go Slow!'"

Two children were overheard arguing in the school playground.

Boy 1: "My dad's a better driver than your dad."

Boy 2: "No he isn't. My dad has gone on a police driving course and is a much better driver than your dad!"

Boy 1: "Okay. Okay. Well my mum is better looking than your mum."

Boy 2: "Well you've got my there. My dad says the same thing."

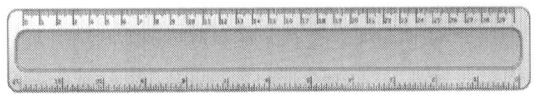

Stephen: "I don't want to go to school today. They all hate me. They call me names and poke fun at me, it's terrible."

Kate: "Come on now, pull yourself together. You've got to go in, you're the Head Teacher."

There are three graduating students applying for the same job. One is a mathematician, one a statistician and one an accountant.

The interviewing committee first calls in the mathematician. They say "We have only one question. What is 500 plus 500?" The mathematician, without hesitation, says "1000." The committee sends him out and calls in the statistician.

When the statistician comes in, they ask the same question. The statistician ponders the question for a moment, and then answers "1000... I'm 95% confident." He is then also thanked for his time and sent on his way.

When the accountant enters the room, he is asked the same question: "What is 500 plus 500?" The accountant replies, "What would you like it to be?"

They hire the accountant.

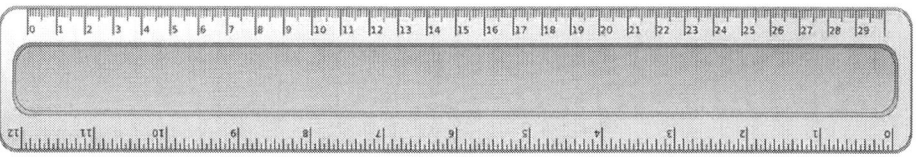

Did you hear about the science teacher who mixed oxygen and magnesium together? OMg!

Teacher: "What is irony?"
Student: "Irony is when something has the chemical symbol Fe."

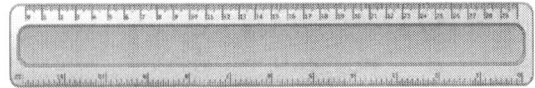

"If there are any idiots in the room, will they please stand up" said the sarcastic teacher. After a long silence, one student rose to his feet.

"Now then mister, why do you consider yourself an idiot?" enquired the teacher with a sneer.

"Well, actually I don't," said the student, "but I hate to see you standing up there all by yourself."

Teacher: "I've had to send you to the Head Teacher every day this week. What do you have to say for yourself?"

Student: "I'm glad it's Friday!"

Each lunchtime a teacher would witness some older kids teasing a younger boy for being stupid. They would offer him a choice between £1 and 50p and watch as he'd always pick the 50p. This would cause the older boys to laugh at him, declaring "He's so thick, he always picks the 50p because it's bigger!"

Finally the teacher decides to have a word with the younger boy, so she took him to one side. "You know how to count, so you must realise that 100 pence is worth more than 50 pence?"

"Of course I do" replied the boy, "but if I stopped picking the 50p they'd stop giving me the money every day."

.

Tricky Questions

Q: What was the first thing Henry VIII did on coming to the throne?

A: He sat down.

Q: How do you get down from an giraffe?

A: You don't - you get down from a duck.

Q: At what battle did Nelson die?

A: His last one.

Q: What is in the capital of France, is very tall and wobbles?

A: The Trifle Tower.

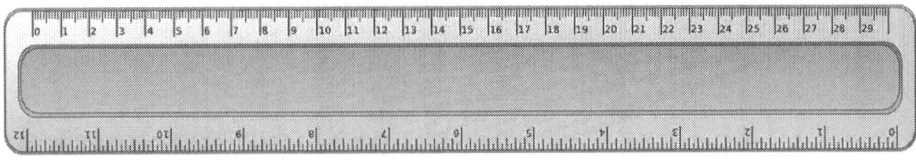

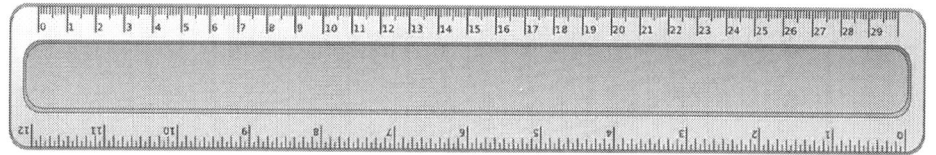

Q: What tables can you eat?

A: Vegetables.

Q: Where does Friday come before Monday?

A: In a dictionary.

Q: What is a four letter word, which ends with 'K' and is another word for 'Intercourse'?

A: Talk.

Q: Why did the student throw his watch out of the school window?

A: He wanted to see time fly.

Q: Why do they never serve beer at a mathematics party?

A: Because you can't drink and derive...

Q: What do you say when you are comforting a grammar fanatic?

A: There, Their, They're.

Q: Why did the student take a ladder to school?

A: Because he was going to high school!

Q: How does the guy who drives the snowplough get to work in the mornings?

Q: What does a dog do that a man steps into?

A: Pants.

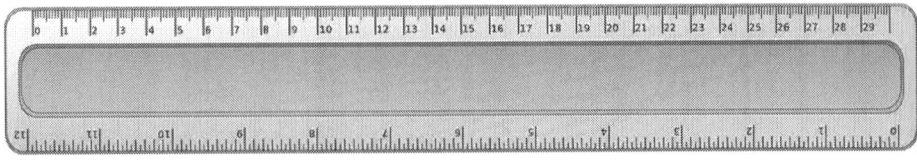

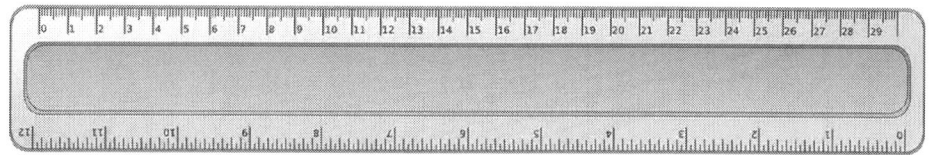

Q: What's starts with a C and ends with a T, is hairy, oval, delicious and contains thin whitish liquid?

A: Coconut.

Q: Why are the Middle Ages sometimes called the Dark Ages?

A: Because there were so many knights.

Q: What's a teacher's favourite nation?

A: Expla-nation.

Q: Why didn't the skeleton go to the school dance?

A: He didn't have anybody to take. (any BODY).

Q: If H20 is water what is H204?

A: Drinking, bathing, washing, swimming. . .

Q: What did one maths book say to the other?

A: Don't bother me I've got my own problems!

Q: What goes in hard and pink then comes out soft and sticky?

A: Bubblegum.

Q: What happened to the plant in maths class?

A: It grew square roots.

Q: Why did the cross-eyed teacher lose her job?

A: Because she couldn't control her pupils?

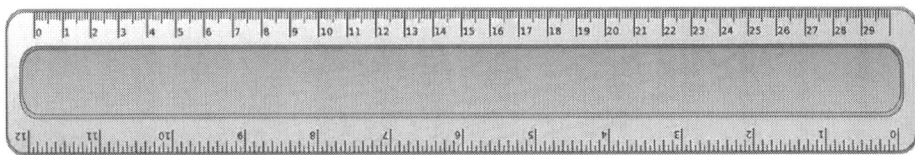

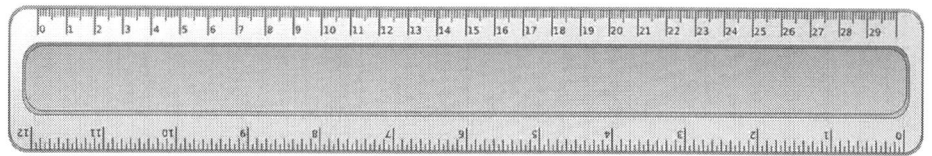

Q: What kind of school do you find on a mountain top?

A: High school.

Q: Why couldn't the mobius strip enrol at the school?

A: They required an orientation.

Q: How did the geography student drown?

A: His grades were below C-level.

Q: What does a mathematician do to cure constipation?

A: He works it out with a pencil.

Q: Why was the maths text book so unhappy?

A: Because it always had lots of problems.

Q: If it's zero degrees outside today and it's supposed to be twice as cold tomorrow, how cold is it going to be?

Q: What's a maths teacher's favourite sum?

A: Summer!

Q: A finger goes in me. You fiddle with me when you're bored. The Best Man always has me first. What am I?

A: Wedding Ring.

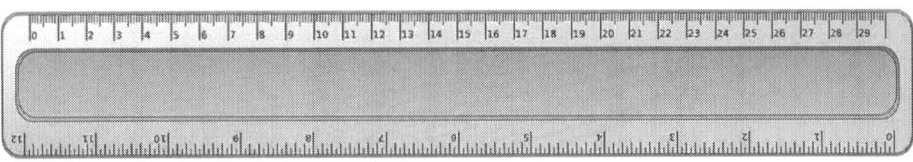

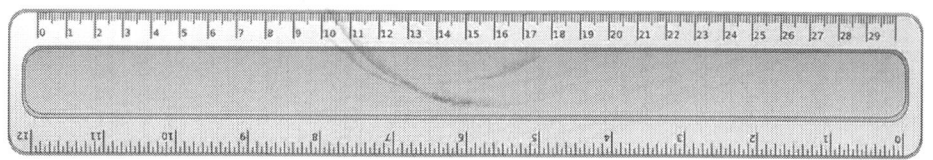

Q: What is the centre of gravity?

A: The letter "V".

Q: Why don't you teach arithmetic in the jungle?

A: Because if you add 4+4 you get ate!

Q: Why don't you teach subtraction in the jungle?

A: Because there are too many adders.

Q: Why is 6 afraid of 7?

A: Because 7 8 9.

Q: What is a chalkboard's favourite drink?

A: Hot chalk-olate!

Q: Why doesn't glue stick to the inside of its bottle?

Q: What is 5Q + 5Q?

A: 10Q ..... and You're Welcome!

Q: How did the maths teacher propose to his fiancée?

A: With a polynomial ring!

Q: What's the longest word in the dictionary?

A: Rubber-band -- because it stretches.

Q: If H2O is the formula for water, what is the formula for ice?

A: H2O cubed.

Q: How does Juliet maintain a constant body temperature?

A: Romeostasis.

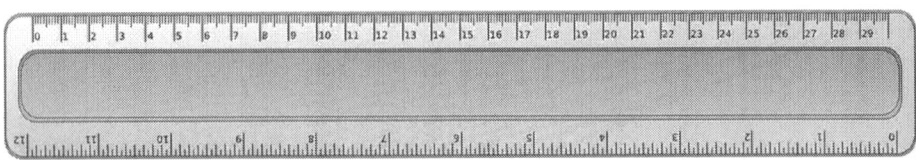

Q: What happened when the teacher tied his pupils shoe laces together?

A: They all went on a class trip.

Q: Why don't farts graduate from high school?

A: Because they always end up getting expelled!

Q: Why did the science teacher go to the tanning salon?

A: Because he was a paleontologist.

Q: Why wasn't the geometry teacher at school?

A: Because she sprained her angle.

Q: Why did the teacher marry the janitor?

A: Because he swept her off her feet!

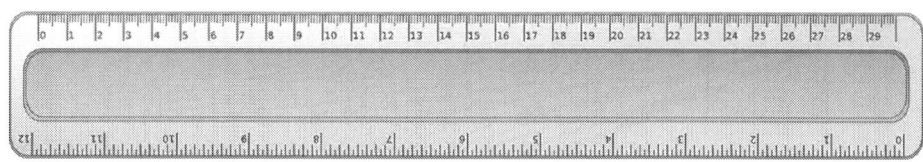

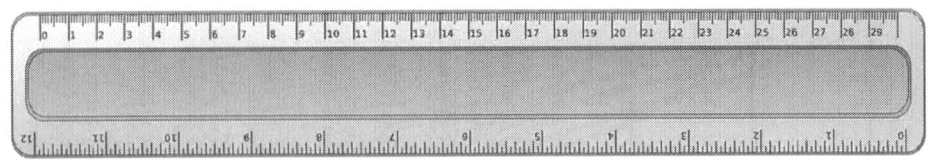

Q: Why did the giraffe get bad grades at school?

A: He had his head in the clouds.

Q: What is the difference between a Ph.D. in mathematics and a large pizza?

A: A large pizza can feed a family of four.

Q: What do you call a music teacher with problems?

A: A trebled man.

Q: What is the shortest month?

A: May, it only has three letters.

Q: What do you know about Red China?

A: I know it will clash with a green tablecloth.

Q: What is the fastest way to determine the sex of a chromosome?

A: Pull down its genes.

Q: Did you hear they're changing the flooring in primary schools?

A: They're calling it infant-tile!

Q: What gets white as it gets dirty?

A: A chalkboard.

Q: Why did the music teacher need a ladder?

A: To reach the high notes.

Q: What do you call the leader of a biology gang?

A: The Nucleus.

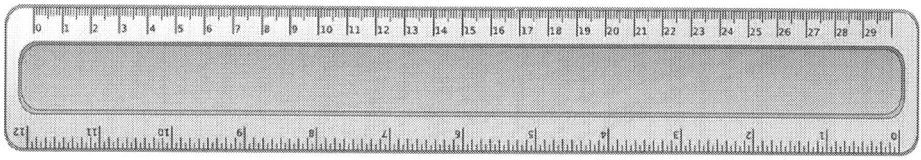

Q: Name a bus you can never enter?

A: A syllabus.

Q: Why do chemistry professors like to teach about ammonia?

A: Because it's basic material.

Q: If you got £20 from 10 people, what do you get?

A: A new bike.

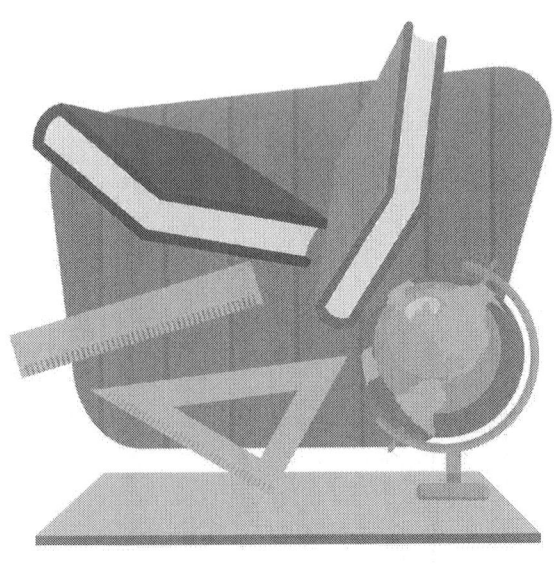

HOMEWORK HOWLERS

Student: "Sir?"

Teacher: "Yes."

Student: "Would you punish me for something I didn't do?"

Teacher: "Of course not."

Student: "I didn't do my homework."

Teacher: "Billy, your homework essay entitled 'My Dog' is exactly the same as your brother's. Did you copy it?"

Billy: "No, Mrs. White. It's the same dog!"

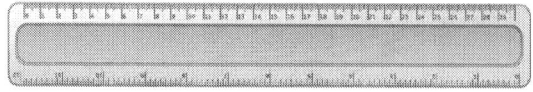

Students Homework Theory: If school isn't a place to sleep then home isn't a place to study.

Teacher: "If a sheep gives you lamb and a pig gives you ham, what does a cow give you?"

Student: "HOMEWORK!"

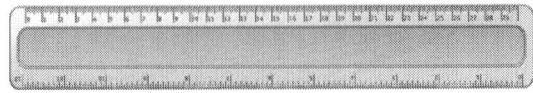

John: "Knock, knock."

Rick: "Who's there?"

John: "Gladys."

Rick: "Gladys, who?"

John: "Gladys the summer - no homework!"

My teacher pointed his ruler at me after I forgot to do my homework and said, "At the end of this ruler there is an idiot."

I got in trouble after asking which end.

STAFFROOM JOKES

These naughty jokes are for adults only.

Student to his teacher: "Are birds made from metal?"

Teacher: "No. What on earth made you ask that?"

Student: "It's just that I overheard my dad say that he'd like to screw the bird next door."

Student to his teacher: "Can chickens grow to 3 or 4 feet?"

Teacher: "No, ostriches do but chickens are only about 1 foot tall. What made you ask that?"

Student: "It's just that I overheard my mum say that she'd like to ride the neighbours cock."

A teacher was finishing his class and started talking about tomorrow's final exam. He said there would be no excuses for not showing up tomorrow, barring a dire medical emergency.

One smart ass, male student said, "What about extreme sexual exhaustion?" And the whole classroom burst into laughter.

After the laughter had subsided the teacher glared at the student and said, "Sorry that's not an excuse, you can always use your other hand to write."

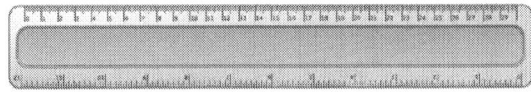

Wife in the bedroom: "Let's role-play tonight."

Husband: "Okay."

Wife: "You be a teacher."

The husband gets out of bed and starts the leave the room.

Wife: "Where are you going?"

Husband: "Do you have any idea how much paperwork I've got to do? And I've got to mark class 8's homework for the morning."

During one of her daily classes, a teacher was trying to teach good manners and asked her students the following question:

"Clive, if you were on a date having dinner with a nice young lady, how would you tell her that you have to go to the bathroom?"

Clive said, "Just a minute I have to go pee."

The teacher responded by saying, "That would be rude and impolite. What about you Paul, how would you say it?"

Paul said, "I am sorry, but I really need to go to the bathroom. I'll be right back."

"That's better," replied the teacher "but it's still not very nice to say the word bathroom at the dinner table. And you, Steven, can you use your brain for once and show us your good manners?"

Steven thought for a minute and then said "I would say: Darling, may I please be excused for a moment? I have to shake hands with a very dear friend of mine, whom I hope to introduce to you after dinner."

A teacher asked for time off because his wife was going to have a baby. The following day the Head Teacher asked him what it was, a boy or a girl?

"Too early to say," replied the teacher, "It'll be another 9 months before we know the answer to that."

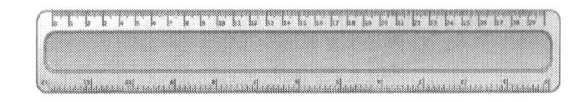

Q: What is Grammar?

A: The difference between knowing your sh*t, and knowing you're sh*t.

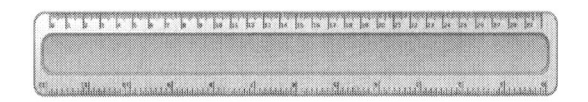

Q: What's the difference between a retired prostitute and school?

A: School still sucks!

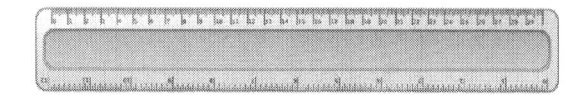

On Monday the teacher asked her pupils to tell the class what they did at the weekend.

Timmy stood up and said "I watched the bull f**king a cow at the farm."

The teacher, embarrassed replied "Thank you Timmy, but perhaps in future you could try not to be so explicit."

The next week the teacher asked the pupils again what they had done at the weekend.

Timmy stands up and this time says "I watched the bull surprising a cow at the farm."

"Well done Timmy," said the teacher "you remembered what I told you last week about your language."

"Well the cow was very surprised" replied Timmy, "as the bull was f**king a horse this time".

A schoolboy walks into a pub and asked for a pint of beer and a cigar.

"Hang on a second" smiled the barmaid, "do you want to get me into trouble?"

"Not at the moment," replied the boy, "I just want my beer and cigar."

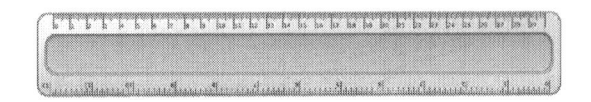

At the end of a biology lesson the teacher points to a girl who has spent the entire time staring out the window and asks, "You girl, what part of the body becomes 10 times its normal size when stimulated?"

The girl goes red with embarrassment and refuses to answer. Eventually another pupil puts his hand up and says "The iris of the eye, Sir."

"Correct," replies the teacher, then turns to the girl and says "Young lady, your refusal to answer my question indicates 3 things. Firstly, you haven't been listening to my lesson. Secondly, you have a dirty mind. And finally, you are going to be very disappointed."

A New Yorker was visiting Oxford University, and was lost. He stopped a student and asked, "Do you know where the library is at?"
"I sure do," replied the student, "But, you know, you're not supposed to end sentences with a preposition."
"A what?"
"Prepositions. You ended your sentence with an 'at', which you aren't supposed to do."
"Oh, okay," said the New Yorker, "Do you know where the library is at, asshole?"

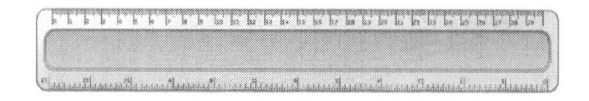

Little Billy returns home from school and says he got an F in arithmetic.
"Why?" asks the father.
"The teacher asked 'How much is 2x3?' and I said '6'"
"But that's right!"
"Then she asked me 'How much is 3x2?'"
"What's the f*cking difference?"
"That's exactly what I said!"

The teacher brings a statue of Venus into class and asks, "What do you like best about it, class? Let's start with you, Peter."

"The artwork," says Peter.

"Very good. And you, Michael?"

"Her t*ts!" says Michael.

"Michael, get out! Go stand in the hall," responds the teacher with disgust. "And now you, Chris?"

"Okay, Okay, I'm leaving, teacher, I'm leaving..." replied Chris.

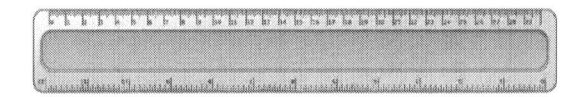

The teacher asks Jimmy to use the word 'definitely' in a sentence.

Jimmy replies, "Teacher, do farts have lumps in them?"

The Teacher says, "Of course not Jimmy, now answer my question", to which Jimmy replies, "Then I have definitely shit my pants."

One day, during a grammar lesson, the teacher asked for a show of hands for who could use the word "beautiful" in the same sentence twice.

First, she called on little Katie, who responded with, "My father bought my mother a beautiful dress and she looked beautiful in it." "Very good, Katie," replied the teacher.

She then called on Trevor. "My mommy planned a beautiful banquet and it turned out beautifully, he said. "Excellent, Trevor!"

Then, the teacher called on Jimmy. "Last night, at the dinner table, my sister told my father that she was pregnant, and he said, 'Beautiful, f**king beautiful!'"

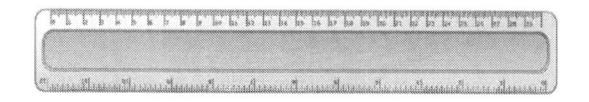

The teacher asked, "Why have you brought your cat to school?"
Student replies (crying), "I heard daddy tell mummy, I'm eating that p*ssy when the kids leave!"

A teacher asks her students to give her a sentence with the word "fascinate" in it.

A little girl says, "I find Space really fascinating." The teacher says, "No, I said, fascinate."

Another little girl says, "There's so much fascination when it comes to sea life."

The teacher again says, "No, the word is fascinate."

Jimmy yells from the back of the room, "My mum has such big boobs that she can only fasten eight of the 10 buttons on her shirt."

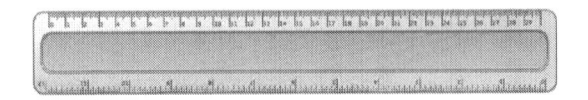

(1) Say "Eye"
(2) Spell the word "Map"
(3) Say "Ness".

Teacher: "Why did you laugh?"

Student: "I saw a strap of your bra."

Teacher: "Get out! Don't come to class for the next week."

Shortly afterwards another boy laughs and the teacher asks: "Why did you laugh?"

Student: "I saw both straps of your bra."

Teacher: "Get out! Don't come to class for the next month."

The teacher bends over to pick up some chalk and Jimmy gets up and starts walking out of the class with his bags.

Teacher: "Why are you leaving?"

Jimmy: "With what I just saw I think my school days are over."

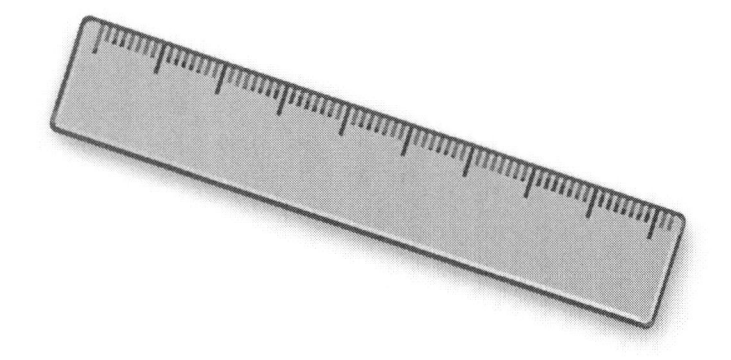

EXAM GIGGLES

In an exam the answer to the problem was "log(1+x)". Chris copied the answer from the student next to him, but didn't want to make it obvious that he was cheating, so he changed the answer slightly, to "timber(1+x)".

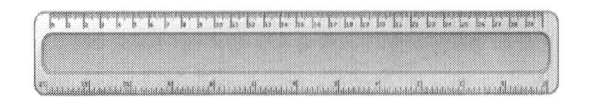

Student: "I don't think I deserved zero on this test."

Teacher: "I agree, but that's the lowest mark I could give you!"

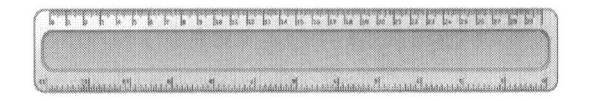

Teacher: "You copied from Fred's exam paper didn't you?"

Student: "How did you know?"

Teacher: "Fred's paper says 'I don't know' to question 3 and you have put 'Me, neither'!"

SCHOOL: 2 + 2 = 4.
HOMEWORK: 2 + 4 + 2 = 8.
EXAM: Matthew has 4 apples, his train is 7 minutes early, calculate the sun's mass.

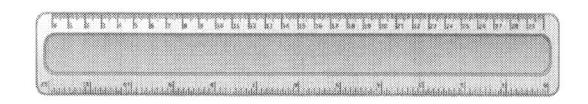

"I've just had the most awful time," said a boy to his friends. "First I got angina pectoris, then arteriosclerosis. Just as I was recovering, I got psoriasis. They gave me hypodermics, and to top it all, tonsillitis was followed by appendectomy."

"Wow! How did you pull through?" sympathised his friends.

"I don't know, just lucky I guess" the boy replied, "It's definitely the toughest spelling test I've ever had."

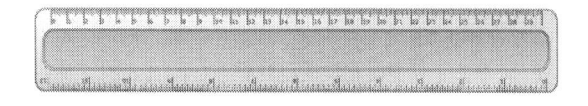

Teacher: "Megan, why are you doing your multiplication test on the floor?"

Megan: "You said we had to do it without using tables!"

Son: "Hey, Mom, I got a hundred in school today!"

Mum: "That's great. What in?"

Son: "A 40 in Reading and a 60 in Spelling."

Mum: "What did you do at school today?"

Son: "We did a guessing game."

Mum: "But I thought you were having a maths exam."

Son: "That's right!"

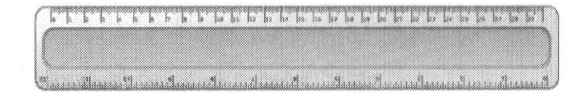

Tim's parents were very disappointed in the grades that he brought home from school. "The only consolation I can find in these awful grades," lamented the father, "is that I know he never cheated during his exams."

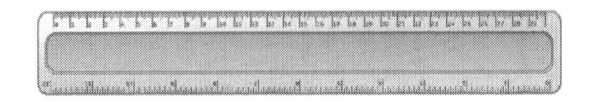

Teacher: "I hope I didn't see you looking at Maria's exam."

Student: "I sure hope you didn't, either!"

THE THREEE R's

Teacher pointing at a student: "Please name two pronouns."

Student: "Who? Me?"

Teacher: "Correct."

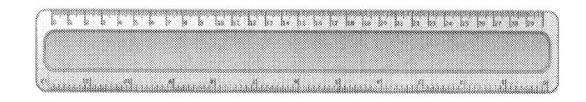

Three intransitive verbs walk into a bar. They sit. They Drink. They Leave.

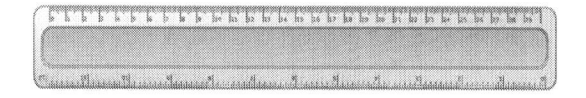

A comma splice walks into a bar, it has a drink and then leaves.

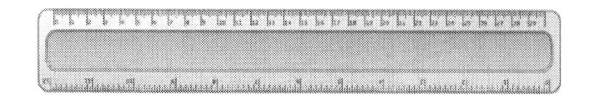

A dangling modifier walks into a bar. After finishing a drink, the bartender asks it to leave.

The past, the present, and the future walked into a bar. It was tense.

A synonym ambles into a pub.

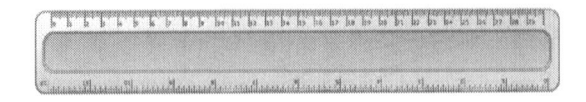

David: "What happened to your girlfriend, that really cute maths student?"
Rory: "She's no longer is my girlfriend. I caught her cheating on me."
David: "I can't believe that she cheated on you!"
Rory: "Well, a couple of nights ago I called her on the phone, and she told me that she couldn't talk as she was in bed wrestling with three unknowns..."

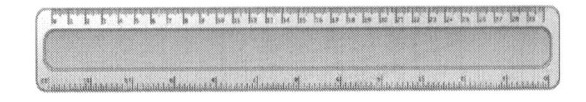

Maths teacher: "A man from Los Angeles drove toward New York at 250 miles per hour and a man from New York drove toward Los Angeles at 150mph Where did they meet?"
Student: "In jail?"

Son: "My teacher says I have to write more clearly."
Mum: "Well that sounds like a reasonable suggestion."
Son: "No, it's not. Then she'll know I can't spell."

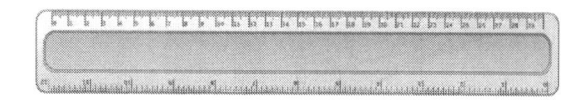

Teacher: "Can anyone give me a sentence with a direct object?"
Student: "You are pretty."
Teacher: "What's the direct object?"
Student: "A good report card."

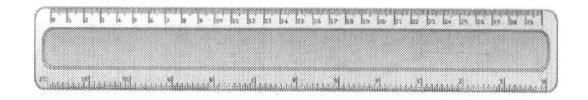

David: "My English teacher is so pedantic."

Mick: "Why's that?"

David: "I said to him the other day 'Can I ask you two questions' and he replied 'Yes, what's the second question.'"

The teacher asks Jimmy if he knows his numbers. "Yes," he says "My daddy taught me."

"Can you tell me what comes after three?" she asked.

"Four," answers Jimmy.

"What comes after six?"

"Seven," answers Jimmy.

"Very good," says the teacher. "Your father did a very fine job. One final question what comes after ten?"

"A jack," answers Jimmy

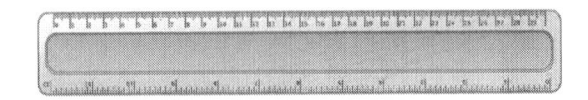

Student: "What's it like being drunk?"
Teacher: "See those 6 desks? A drunk person would see 12."
Student: "There are only 3 desks."

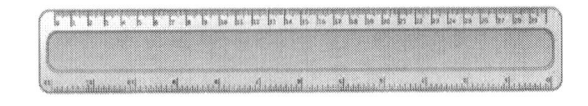

A maths teacher is the type of person who will tell someone who has their feet in the oven and their head in the refrigerator, that on average they are actually very comfortable.

ONE-LINERS

If teachers are so smart, why are they still in school?

If sleep is really good for the brain, then why is it not permitted in school?

Teacher to unruly student: "I suppose you could be worse. You could be twins."

If a picture is worth a thousand words, then why shouldn't we judge a book by its cover?

To steal ideas from one person is plagiarism. To steal ideas from many is research.

That awkward moment when you go to a new school and don't get a vampire boyfriend.

Teacher to unruly student: "I can read you like a book, it's just unfortunate that I can't shut you up like one."

Two things you can learn in school: Texting without looking and teamwork on tests.

C.L.A.S.S. = Come Late And Start Sleeping

M.A.T.H. = Mental Abuse to Humans

S.C.H.O.O.L. = Seven Crappy Hours Of Our Life

Teacher to student: "How many millions of times have I told you not to exaggerate?"

My favourite school book? 'Time to go home' by Wendy Belrings.

Student: "My history teacher is so old, that when he orders a three-minute egg they make him pay up front."

Janitors don't die, they just kick the bucket.

Teacher to unruly student: "Someday you'll go too far - and I hope you stay there."

PLAYGROUND GROANS

Q: What do you call a friendly school?

A: Hi School!

Q: Why were the teacher's eyes crossed?

A: She couldn't control her pupils.

Teachers always tell us to follow our dreams....BUT yet they don't let us sleep in class.

Q: Why did the teacher marry the janitor?

A: Because he swept her off her feet.

Q: What is the Great Depression?

A: When you get a bad grade in history.

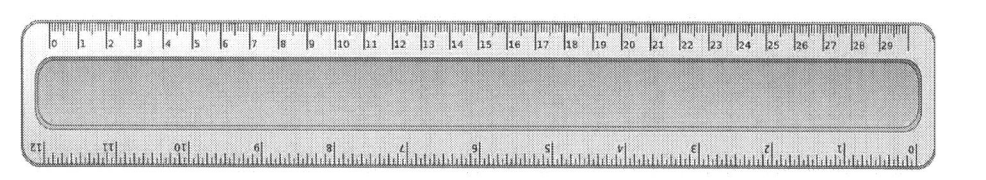

Teacher: "Why were you late?"

Student: "Sorry, teacher, I overslept."

Teacher: "You mean you need to sleep at home as well?"

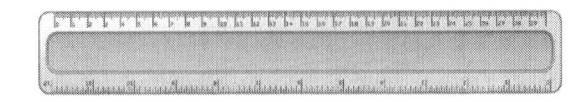

Q: What would happen if you took the school bus home?

A: The police would make you bring it back!

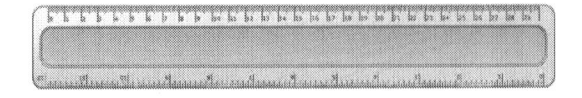

Q: What's the longest piece of furniture in the school?

A: The multiplication table.

Q: What do you get when you cross a teacher with a vampire?

A: Lots of blood tests.

Q: Why was the students report card all wet?

A: Because it was below C (sea) level.

Q: Why did Johnny take a ruler to bed?

A: Because he wanted to see how long he slept!

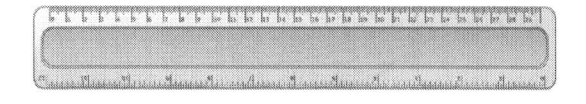

Q: Why don't you see giraffes in primary school?

A: Because they're all in HIGH School.

Q: Who should be your best friend at school?

A: Your princi-pal!

Q: How do you spell Hard Water with 3 letters?

A: ICE!

Teacher: "What are the seasons?"

Student: "Salt, pepper, ginger..."

Son: "I can't go to school today."

Father: "Why not?"

Son: "I don't feel well."

Father: "Where don't you feel well?"

Son: "In school!"

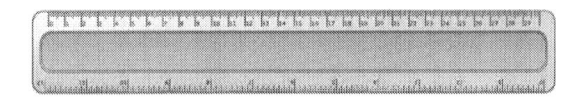

Helen: "I bet school easier for cave people."

Julia: "Why's that?"

Helen: "Because there was no history to study!"

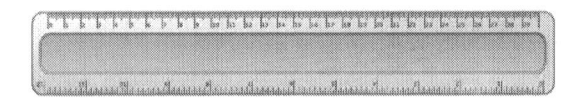

Pete: "Why was the teacher wearing sunglasses to school?"

Mike: "Why?"

Pete: "She had lots of bright students!"

Lee: "What's the king of all school supplies?"

Phil: "I don't know. What?"

Lee: "The ruler."

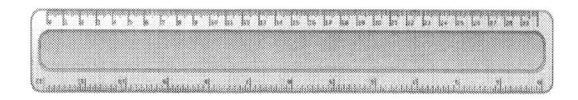

Q: What kind of school do you go to if you're an ice cream man?

A: Sundae school.

Q: What kind of school do you go to if you're a giant?

A: High school.

Q: What kind of school do you go to if you're a surfer?

A: Boarding school.

Q: What kind of school do you go to if you're King Arthur?

A: Knight school.

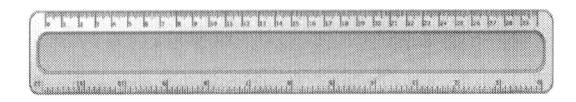

Teacher: "Where are the Great Plains located?"

Student: "At the great airports!"

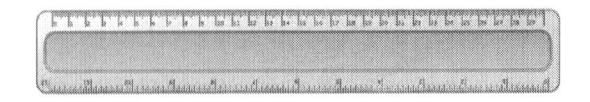

Teacher: "If you had 13 apples, 12 grapes, 3 pineapples and 3 strawberries, what would you have?"

Student: "A delicious fruit salad."

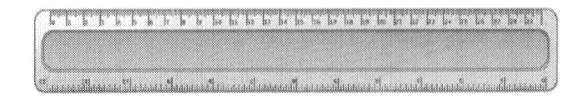

Teacher: "Can you tell us where the Magna Carta was signed?"

Student: "Yes, ma'am. At the bottom."

Pete: "What's the difference between a teacher and a train?"

Owen: "What?"

Pete: "A teacher says, 'Spit out that gum!' whilst a train says, 'Chew! Chew!'"

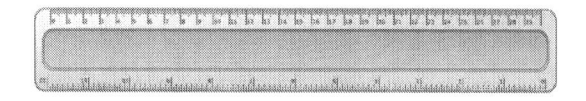

Teacher: "Why will you never be able to work in an orange juice factory?"

Student: "I don't know. Why?"

Teacher: "Because you can't concentrate!"

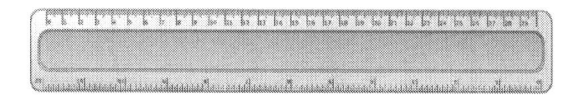

Trevor: "Why do magicians do so well in school?"

Steph: "I don't know. Why?"

Trevor: "They're good at trick questions."

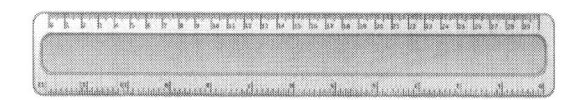

A gym teacher goes to his doctor and says, "My foot really hurts - what should I do?"

The doctor replied "Limp."

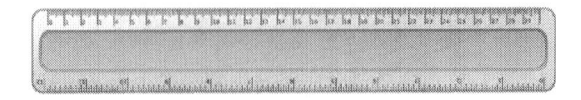

Q: Where do panel-beaters get their education?

A: The school of hard knocks.

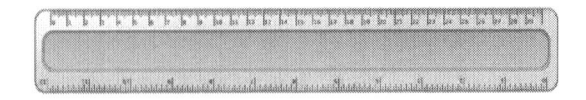

An elderly teacher said to her student "If I say the phrase 'I am beautiful', which tense is that in?"

The student replied, "It's obviously in the past."

Printed in Great Britain
by Amazon